THE NEEDLE HAS LANDED

poems by

ALICIA CALDANARO

Finishing Line Press
Georgetown, Kentucky

THE NEEDLE HAS LANDED

Copyright © 2026 by Alicia Caldanaro
ISBN 979-8-89990-328-1 First Edition
All rights reserved under International and Pan-American Copyright Conventions. No part of this book may be reproduced in any manner whatsoever without written permission from the publisher, except in the case of brief quotations embodied in critical articles and reviews.

ACKNOWLEDGMENTS

"I Looked For Sylvia in the Library," was published in *North Dakota Quarterly*
"That," was published in *Abandoned Mine*, online
"The Garden Layout," was published in *Caesura: Objects in the Mirror*
"The Needle Has Landed: A Tribute to Judy Garland," "Houdini Magic," and "The DJ Poem" were published in *Analecta*. A special thank you to Professor David Dodd Lee for two semesters of Advanced Poetry Writing courses.
"A Time to Heal," was published in *Laurel Review*
"Mrs. Cratchit's Blazing Pudding," was published in *Willow Review*
"I Never Had My Wisdom Teeth Removed," "This Isn't an All-Night Diner," and "Haunted Neon Lights" were published online in *The Writing Disorder. com: A Literary Journal*

All photographs were taken by Alicia Caldanaro, including the front cover yellow swallowtail butterfly who stared at her in her flower garden on the orange tiger lily flower from her mom. The inside photographs include her artwork: Alicia's feet next to her cat, Aslan; and Alicia's sewing; quilting; baking; and gardening with flowers.

Publisher: Leah Huete de Maines
Editor: Christen Kincaid
Cover Art: Alicia Caldanaro
Author Photo: Keegan
Cover Design: Elizabeth Maines McCleavy

Order online: www.finishinglinepress.com
  also available on amazon.com

Author inquiries and mail orders:
Finishing Line Press
PO Box 1626
Georgetown, Kentucky 40324
USA

Contents

Photo of Alicia's feet wearing shoes that complement the color of her nearby cat: Aslan ("The Great Lion") ... 1
I Never Had My Wisdom Teeth Removed ... 2
I Go Antiquing with Frank O'Hara ... 4
Photo of "Library Interior Appliqued Tied Quilt" Made by Alicia ... 5
Photo of "Appliqued Quilt Block, in Memory of Sylvia Plath's poem, 'Balloons'" ... 6
I Looked for Sylvia in the Library ... 7
Photo that includes fun baked goods ... 8
This Isn't an All-Night Diner ... 9
That ... 10
Photo of American Girl doll, "Caroline," wearing Halloween costume Alicia sewed for her daughter with the same name, from McCall's pattern ... 11
An Acknowledgment to the Movie, The Wolf Man (1941) ... 12
The Needle Has Landed: A Tribute to Judy Garland ... 13
Haunted Neon Lights ... 15
Photo of The Monkees fleece fabric with yellow satin blanket binding sewn by Alicia ... 16
Photo of appliqued wall hanging with buttons—sharing the theme of the joy of sewing and flower gardening, sewn by Alicia ... 17
The Garden Layout ... 18
Depictions From Mountain Climbers ... 19
Photo of Alicia's flowers that she grew, cared for, and arranged and found the Ladies Home Journal-themed container in an antique mall and purchased it to hold this beauty ... 20
Photo of homemade Christmas cookies baked, decorated, displayed, and arranged by Alicia for everyone's enjoyment at her sister Maria's Christmas party ... 21
Mrs. Cratchit's Blazing Pudding ... 22
Houdini Magic ... 23
Persevere Despite the Room's Elephant ... 24
Elevated Art ... 25
Dancing in Front of the Mirror ... 26
A Time to Heal ... 27
Chicken Beaks Are Always Open in Hot Weather ... 29
The DJ Poem ... 30

To all women who are survivors

I NEVER HAD MY WISDOM TEETH REMOVED

If now is not part of the past, why does the past often go back and
forth in my mind
during present moments? It either hangs over my head like a black
cloud or burns like
Jack's fabulous yellow roman candles. Mouths get canker sores and
backs break out in
hives. As the escalator gave my ankles a break from shopping, Santa
Claus looked up
at me, smiled, and waved. Raindrops became a shower. Gene Kelly
gave me his umbrella
and I started dancing. My dance was not as cool as the dance Jenna
Ortega choreographed
and performed herself on *Wednesday*. However, she wears black, I
wear gray, and my
piano teacher told me I was one of her few students who did not
need a metronome. What
is it with my veterinarian who explained to me, *after* she removed
forty percent of my cat's
teeth, that they were rotten because of his poor genetics? She left his
front canines and
incisors, but was that supposed to soothe him and me? I named my
cat Aslan ("The Great
Lion") because he processioned between my two rows of orange
cosmoses where I counted twenty-nine aggressive bumblebees
pollinating in the hot afternoon. A week after Aslan's teeth were
yanked out, an abscess developed under his chin and it burst when I
was on my way out
the door. I padded his open sore till it stopped bleeding, left him in
the house, raced to hear
a poet give a reading, and the day improved. It took a month to *not*
see Aslan's sore mouth
of red inflamed gums. The only item I ever buy in gas stations is pink
bubble gum because
I cannot find it at most grocery stores. My two-year-old niece will
repeatedly watch me
blow bubble gum bubbles. One time Grandma Agnes started at the
crown of my head and

ran her hand gently down the back of my hair while Aunt Ann handed me a chocolate chip cookie. Masking tape would not hold up my poster of Mulder and Scully so Mom gave me duct tape. When I was in second grade, Grandma Rosie gave me my first poetry book, *Marigold Garden* by Kate Greenaway. Aslan left a dead bird on my front step today. No one knows what will happen.

I GO ANTIQUING WITH FRANK O'HARA

We have classic interests. An
                    unbelievably blue sky and radiant
yellow sun
            prompts us to go shopping at the local antique market.
Overwhelmed with crammed junk in seller booths (that we have to
sift through to find the good stuff)—
                            what stands out to us is the
well-written label by the dealer: "Vintage
                            Mid-Century Modern
Mahogany Telephone Gossip Bench." We laugh as we squeeze
together on the cushioned seat. This old-fashioned nostalgic piece
of furniture is held together by the
                            surrounding support of a
lustrous reddish-brown American evergreen tree (which the bench
and the attached table were created from). The dealer has
an eye for display—
            so much so that the rotary telephone placed
on the tabletop beckons us to make
                    imaginary phone calls where
we discuss what makes this bench so
                        inviting—not only does it
offer a welcoming feeling to any
                        entryway, but what visitor
doesn't relish the thought of being able to sit when taking off and
putting on their shoes? The
                authenticity of the bench heartens me
to buy it. Encouraged by Frank and I's amusing conversations, I
immediately discern
            (when my own delightful laughter wakes me
up)—this dream was the first time I *remember* dreaming in color.

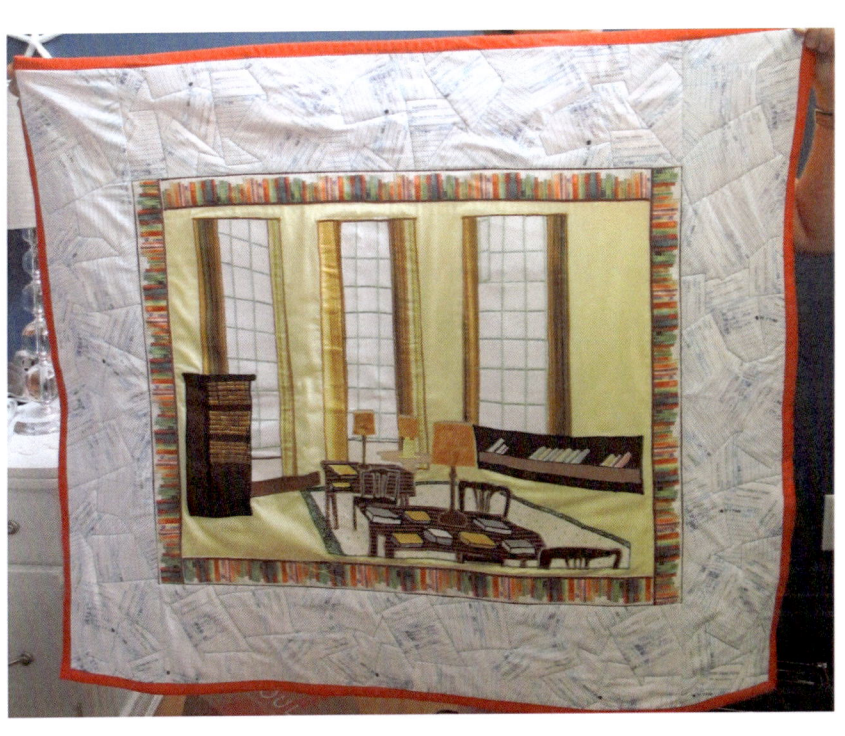

I LOOKED FOR SYLVIA IN THE LIBRARY

A poem inspired by Sylvia Plath's book "Letters Home" (Selected and Edited with Commentary by her mother, Aurelia Schober Plath)

She was hiding on the bookshelf,
Behind her mother's skirt
I had to physically hold the object itself:
The book—

It was a book that had her letters
She constructed diligently
As a form of communication
That encouraged her to be

A love that was sought and shared by the two—
A love between mother and daughter—
A love that subliminally grew—

Sylvia's mother mailed overseas
Something to cheer her daughter and grandchildren
And, also, to appease

These colorful gifts that were mailed produced a light that radiated
For a mother and her children—
Read about it in the poem "Balloons;"—
That Sylvia created!

"If you ever want to make another hit, send some more kitty balloons!" From Sylvia in a letter to her mother, Aurelia Schober Plath, dated December 21, 1962. On page 492 of Plath, Sylvia. Letters Home, Selected and Edited with Commentary by Aurelia Schober Plath, Harper & Row, 1975.

THIS ISN'T AN ALL-NIGHT DINER

I am as mad as Yosemite Sam!
When my feet move forward, the
orchestra gives each stomp a strong
staccato. Take the keys and lock up
my fair lady. You didn't say UNO!
Lonely preparation
and unmelodious response.
See a penny? pick it up!
Too many choices: Pink Lady, Fuji, McIntosh,
Jonagold, Jazz, Golden Delicious,
Honeycrisp, and Granny Smith.
Grandma always said:
better than sliced bread.
Vegetable knife in my right hand.
Band-Aid on my left thumb. Singed
skin from cookie sheets turns into blisters
that change to small, white, and
unerasable marks. Forthcoming book…
still in progress. Distasteful raw carrots were
inaudibly spat out by a rabbit.
Yosemite Sam strained Mel Blanc's voice the most.
I make a mean carrot cake despite it all—

THAT

I don't want to remember that
Or write about that
It doesn't seem right to give any attention at all to that

I have better things to think about—
    Nice things, productive things

Why do I have to remember that?
I shut it out
It was a long time ago
It haunts me sometimes
The media tells me stories that remind me of that—
    The battered women who were victims
I got out a long time ago and I told the social worker that I was a victim
The social worker corrected me and told me that I was a survivor

So, my mind and heart and experience about that
Forces my reluctant hand to write what needs to be known
Because maybe others are experiencing that
Right now
I pick up my pen
And finally,
After many years,
I start to write about that

AN ACKNOWLEDGMENT TO THE MOVIE, *THE WOLF MAN* (1941)

Although they tried awfully hard to do so,
those werewolves
               couldn't
make a pentagram appear on the palm of my
hand.
     After the gypsy woman fortune teller named Maleva
told me about my
              future, more gypsies came to town and
danced on the grave of
               my former self (who was worthy of such
a pagan celebration for strengths of suppressed sadness —). My
imitable spirit survived
               through it all—Always able to
recoup
     because I carry an
antique
         get-up-and-go cane with the talisman of
                            a small
solid silver
         wolf on top of it.

THE NEEDLE HAS LANDED: A TRIBUTE TO JUDY GARLAND

Detroit News, September 29, 1967. What is left is nostalgia—with enough of the special magic to make an evening with Judy Garland an unbelievable experience. It would be easy to say the magic was all in the minds of the beholders. But even the most hardened cynic might wonder if he hadn't caught a twinkle of it himself from this capricious leprechaun on stage. —Bob Carr (Emily R. Coleman, *The Complete Judy Garland*, New York: Harper & Row, 1990, 262).

It's an old sturdy sewing table with a big deep scratch on it like a battle scar.
It holds my sewing machine (with repetitively familiar sounds) that provides the main sense
of control I have in this life. Most of the sounds are soothing and the machine always has
work to do—

Near the end of the process of making a quilt, there's three layers to bind together—
the colorful top for show, the middle with thick batting, and the back that one rarely
looks at. Patience is required—stitching the bulky layers of this quilt together usually
breaks a needle or two. Sometimes it's cumbersome to keep replacing needles.

Like Holden Caulfield's reference to the heaviness of dancing with the statue of liberty: that's how I feel when I drag the heavy table holding the machine across the floor to the window so I can see the natural light.
I prepare to set foot in the land of beauty—

I see the nearby spines of Judy, Elvis, Jimmy (James Dean), Sivvy (Sylvia Plath),
and "The Goose Man" (L. Frank Baum). Before I begin my journey to Oz, wee pieces
of a protective disintegrating paper sleeve fall on the blue rug as I admire the

leprechaun who captured me with her pot of gold on eBay.

I hear the individualistic overture that only lasts four seconds on the shiny black circled
surface of possibilities: a static sound once, but now it is the clear sound of a wave crashing
on the edge of the beach (where the ocean meets the land). Then I hear a quiet orchestra that
Garland's felt presence alone summons. Shy, subtle, and sweet at first, her voice sings to me—

She's gonna love me like nobody's loved me "Come Rain or Come Shine." She crescendos
Harold Arlen's song and I hear a small laugh before she belts out, "Won't that be fine?"—And I've always thought so ever since I was a kid in the '70s—when television yearly aired her movie
that showed her singing the #1 Song of the (20th) Century in Kansas with Toto nearby.

I've got my own needle playing my own song in the background like Winona and the
older beauties in *How to Make an American Quilt*. I have measured, pieced, cut, ironed, pinned,
and sewn all these colorful pieces of fabric together to make my own story. I have ripped
the seams out and started over many times.

But, just for a bit, it's time to turn off the sewing machine and record player. I want to embrace
the quietness because I want to hear my own personal favorite soft sound—the sound the thread makes—when I'm pushing and pulling my hand-held sewing needle through the fabric and tying my own quilt together with my weathered hands that have delicate fingers.

HAUNTED NEON LIGHTS

I knew it was over. I folded the red construction paper
in half, drew half a heart on the fold, and the scissors
were too dull to cut the heart out. Time to move on
because...what were we going to do? Hang out? *No*.
It was time for the sovereign remedies—
I relied on Matt Foley who shouted, "La Dee Frickin' Da!"
in his "van down by the river," and who fell a million
different ways then exclaimed, "Whoops-A-Daisy!"
to cheer me up. I laughed along with Elaine when Jerry
put the Tweety Bird Pez dispenser on top of her purse. I
wanted Kramer to put up a screen door and spray potted
azaleas, and afterwards we'd sit on old lawn chairs from
the 1970s: woven straps of green and white stripes held
together with Phillips screws in the aluminum chair frames.
I wanted to grill hamburgers and roast marshmallows
over charcoal. I could not wait to devour the toasted-to-a-light-
brown (on the outside) and the semi-melted, glossy-sweet
fluff (on the inside) of the marshmallows. You knew I was
better when you did *not* see me crying during *most* of the *Little
House on the Prairie* reruns I binged. You were proud of me
when at the midst of a table d'hôte, I did *not* yodel back to the
lonely goatherd. You laughed when I asked three friends to join
me and we copied the overlapping-legs-walk from The Monkees.
You knew I'd recovered when we watched the flowers growing
by the lamppost that told me it had rhymes for me.

THE GARDEN LAYOUT

I have a window above my kitchen sink where
I see my flower garden outside. I prepare
a whole chicken for roasting. My clothes are kept clean
by an apron that I sewed together
from a *McCall's* pattern. I made my own
bows (pretty embellishments) from
a ribbon with smiling red crabs. I stitched
the bows near my red heart. It seems a shame
to take the potted herb and cut it from its soil
just to make Martha Stewart's lemon roasted
chicken beautiful. I rub the cavity with
salt, stuff the chicken with rosemary and
two halved lemons. My hands are full of
raw chicken, but the view from my window
reminds me I'm Snow White—chickadees, robins,
cardinals, goldfinches, red-winged
blackbirds, and woodpeckers greet me when I
sing. My praying angel statue kneels among my
red tuberous begonias. She is barefoot, more
beauty is behind her—wings that look like lacy
leaves. I do a leaf rubbing over those wings
and the crayons make an imprint with strong veins showing.
New art keeps originating.

DEPICTIONS FROM MOUNTAIN CLIMBERS

As a kid, I took photos when Mom gave me her old
camera—prints atop a pine tree I liked to climb.
The branches were like a ladder: easy
to get to the top. On my way up, I took hold
of the wind-waving pine needles and time
paused as I touched that evergreen—so velvety!

Closing its scales is what keeps seeds safe in a pine cone.
Mom taught me how to *hold one's own*.
Alongside slow vehicles in her funeral procession—
on the way to the cemetery,
with pine trees behind them—fifteen men
took off their hard hats in commemoration
and placed the hats by their hearts as we drove to bury
Mom, who would have loved to witness such reverence…Amen.

MRS. CRATCHIT'S BLAZING PUDDING

I reach out my hands for a Christmas dance.
The fiddler plays "Sir Roger de Coverley"
while Mr. and Mrs. Fezziwig perform the
English slip jig dance of exultant merriment.
Dickens brought me Scrooge, reborn from
shade that shelters—I embrace it and become
hallowed grace, soother of present and future.
Beloved faces always shine brightly, no matter
how dark the room.

HOUDINI MAGIC

    You are sorting mail. Naomi, Elaine, Jan, Mary, Debbie, and Joyce pop in and, as usual, address to me the topic of is-this-a-fresh-pot-of-coffee? Your
nod that only I see
                from behind towers of boxes that block my vision
to the coffee pot that is
20 feet away lets me know you and I occupy the same space
                                        where there
are two corners: one where I'm putting in my blood, sweat, and tears
and the other where you are happily
in my
       peripheral vision: One particular moment the chicken coop is
empty so I tell you an
outstretched-arms-open-hands-TA-DAAAAH! worthy story: "My
dad showed me how to find the
smelly leak in the dump that I live in: he rubbed dish soap on the
metal tube from my gas dryer
and it bubbled. You must have *MacGyver* skills when you're on your
own." Your rebuttal: "Too
bad people aren't really like *MacGyver*." We start to pour our hearts
out—great dogs
                                      protecting us when
we were down in the dumps—yours, a German Shephard; mine, a
Blue Merle Collie. Your parents
were divorced over 14 years ago and your heavy sigh says it all
                              right before you tell the part where she still
has wedding photos on display with your womanizing cop dad. Your
eye
catches mine and
                      you roll out the red carpet. We amaze each other
with sleight of hand and
abracadabras only understandable to us.

PERSEVERE DESPITE THE ROOM'S ELEPHANT

I went to the circus and saw
an elephant balancing its four feet on a large ball

a spectacle that could not be ignored.
I find myself thinking of that elephant often…

Perhaps there's a period of years it takes to experience what should
have been obvious.
Like when I was a little kid

And Mom took me and my brothers and sisters
To pick blackberries in the woods.

Summers were hot and we'd be batting away bugs,
Mom as our leader, who'd made a path, pushing away prickers and
vines,

snapping branches, her white safari hat
like a lantern we followed

when *voilà!* We're in this dreamy patch
of tall green grass and the blackberries are on the bright sunny edge
of it—

shining at us like a fairy godmother put them there for us
to pick

So we kids each grab for our first blackberry
And my index finger gets in the way

of the Sticker
That's hidden by the pretty green leaves on the blackberry bush.

A tiny bead of blood wells up on the end my index finger.
And Mom tells me to put pressure on it and we keep on picking
blackberries.

ELEVATED ART

I love *Peanuts* comic strips by Charles M. Schulz ("Sparky"), who told Charlie Rose
how he read Andrew Wyeth's biography and thought how Wyeth
Really gets to do what
he wants. I look at pictures first (like a toddler who does not know how to read yet)
to make up my own mind.

My first impression of Wyeth's *Christina's World*: a woman lying upwards on a
hill of healthy grass while propping herself up with her hands and thinking about
what *could* happen—looking for something good at home in the distance and resting to
get her second wind before continuing to run there.

Too bad the painting does not show her eyes because like Pippin's first impression of
Treebeard's eyes, I could see ages of memory in Sparky's courteousness. I looked up two
more things—Christina Olson was a hermit who was also a disabled friend of Wyeth's.
Rather than use a wheelchair, she preferred to drag herself around.

People live such a long time, crawling from one place to a better place. A huge branch
broke from a towering old tree and the bench that I placed in my backyard is bent
from it. Personalities have fugitive pieces that are surprising. I am teaching myself
the whole-souled language of Old Entish.

DANCING IN FRONT OF THE MIRROR

Lunches, gifts galore—
not the kind where money resides. Sustainability is a tall glass
of water with lots of ice. A flare for the interpersonal,

gestures of empathy, lucky to have listening space—
relaxed eyes and relaxed voices. Years pass and a
movie theater shows *E.T. the Extra-Terrestrial* again.

Afterwards, the usher smiles and amusingly questions
our watery eyes. Often in a tunnel…
Sometimes I feel

goosebumps on my arms and I hear blue butterflies
in my stomach. I want savory, delicious Saganaki—Opa! —
because of the quick shine (yellow, orange, and blue)—

I cannot move my wide-open eyes away from such
burning zeal. Only a few undoubtedly notice
the title written on my mixtape: Fortitude.

It goes by fast. An amusement park leap
in the glow all ablaze—
Reviver, restorer…always the brilliant illuminator of a fireplace.

A TIME TO HEAL

I had Halloween masks that were plastic in elementary school
in the 1970s back then you just bought a mask with the skinny
elastic string that wrapped tight around the back of your head
and it usually broke, but anyway, the top of the box lid
was see-through (the mask and part of the cheap fabric costume
was in view) so you knew what you were buying but you didn't care
because you just wanted to go trick or treating that's what they sold
at stores like Ben Franklin   (why did they call it "Ben
Franklin"?)
it was more like a small version of Kmart, but Kmart disappeared
years ago too I know most of the *Bewitched* episodes by heart
like the 2-part episode about Ben Franklin noting his marvelous
accomplishments and Aunt Clara, sincere and funny, was in that
one,
oh, it's just a given that Elizabeth Montgomery as Samantha
never fails to be delightful and lovely when my daughter was born
I was lonely for something familiar, so I bought the first 6 seasons
on DVD and they kept me company and cheered me up as I learned
how to be a new stay-at-home mom with a newborn one time
when my daughter was four, she was scared and woke me up
at 2 a.m. I put my arm around her as we sat up and watched
the funniest *Bewitched* episode the one where Samantha's
Uncle Arthur makes Darrin think he gave him special powers
so Darrin thinks he can play a trick on Endora and Uncle Arthur
has Darrin sing, "Yagga zuzzi, yagga zuzzi, yagga zuzzi zim" ending
with a duck call and a cowbell and I wish I could talk to someone
on the phone who, like Paul Lynde, felt that making people laugh
was the most important thing a person could do because I'd really
like to laugh the kind of laugh that makes you cry like when I read
the story in *Me Talk Pretty One Day* by David Sedaris how his sister
got dressed up in this costume suit and their father didn't know
it was fake I laughed so hard I cried that was the last time
that happened to me I hope someday it happens again even though
my smile hurt and my stomach ached from laughing it was worth
every second but last summer-through-winter sucked and I can't
remember 3 seasons sucking so bad I looked as white as a ghost

most days the only thing that consoled me was watching Sam and
Dean
make salt circles for the innocent to sit within while they fought off
ghosts now at least I'm done vegging out for a while I still have
almost 1 ½ seasons left of *Supernatural* to watch after binging
most of it last summer through winter on Netflix; however, this year,
off and on, I'm watching something else trying to save the episodes
for a rainy day I'm hoarding them moving slowly snow falling on my
driveway because each one of those episodes will at least be new to
me now

CHICKEN BEAKS ARE ALWAYS OPEN IN HOT WEATHER

Vanessa is a forty-year-old woman who lives in a shack in Potter's Field. She loves remodeling dollhouses, but does not like personal questions. Vanessa wants to learn how to play the piano because it makes her happy to hear Waz, who is a struggling musician, play all of the pianos so beautifully at the music store where they are employed. She finds humor in the fact that in order to look professional at his gigs, Waz saves money by buying dead men's new-looking suits donated to resale shops. Vanessa's music store tasks include helping customers and cleaning each individual ivory piano key with new cloth baby diapers sprayed with Windex. Most evenings at home, she can be found painting dollhouse rooms different colors. Vanessa once visited a crayon factory with Mister Rogers where she used her photographic memory to record colors she knew would go well together in the rooms of her miniature world. She gets discouraged with her life because she is rarely able to remove splinters in her fingers with tweezers—she has to use needles. She gets sick when she forgets to put the hood up on her sweatshirt in cold weather. She went to the county fair and noticed each chicken had an individual cage, but their water dishes were empty. She filled each water dish and alleviated their thirst. And they stopped panting. And Vanessa finally realized she was much more than useful.

THE DJ POEM

As I stared at the second hand of the clock above the radio control board, I had the
next record cued up. Even though the higher-ups gave me weekend graveyard shifts,
dead air never existed when I was the disc jockey. I announced my name, the local
weather forecast, and the call letters of the station right before Rhett Akins broke into
his vocal on "That Ain't My Truck." As I checked the program log and stacked
commercials to play on the air, I noticed a dramatic pause between each ring on the
rotary telephone's call for me to answer…the caller was a classmate acquaintance from
elementary through high school and after she told me who she was, I said: "Shelly,
please hold on a minute, I'm going to play 'American Pie,' it's an old DJ trick when
we need extra time to run to the bathroom." (I had to play a long song so we could talk
before I had to be on the air again). It had been nine years since we graduated from
high school. I flashed back to us in the same elementary school class––at a class field trip,
at the Jasper-Pulaski Fish and Wildlife Area, watching prehistoric-looking Sandhill Cranes
in the shallow marshes…a memory came back to me like a bolt out of the blue: guitar,
drum, and excessive "Oi, Oi, Oi's" from AC/DC's "T.N.T." blared from the cassette
player that another kid in our class, sneaky Brian, ignited—much to the teacher's
surprise…Shelly and I laughed about that and in the seconds before the song was over,
she said to me: "Bye-bye, so nice to hear your voice."

Alicia Caldanaro was born in Valparaiso, Indiana, in 1968 and graduated from Saint Joseph's College in Rensselaer, Indiana, in 1990. She studied at Indiana University in Bloomington, where she earned her Master of Library Science degree and "Specialization in Special Collections" certificate that included working on the manuscripts of Athol Fugard.

Her work has appeared in *Plath Profiles, Abandoned Mine, North Dakota Quarterly, Caesura, Analecta, Laurel Review, Willow Review,* and *The Writing Disorder.com: A Literary Journal.*

Academic librarianship has been her forte regarding work experiences. Alicia took Advanced Poetry Writing courses at Indiana University South Bend in 2023 which encouraged her lifelong love of writing poetry.

This is Alicia's first book of poetry, and it includes complementary photographs of her artwork. The reader will experience a conversational quality interspersed with the use of references, especially to recognizable pop culture. Alicia's ability to weave the past into the present is charming and playful but sometimes undergirded by something slightly sinister—A cry from a superheroine from a world so actually depicted it is no doubt home.

www.ingramcontent.com/pod-product-compliance
Lightning Source LLC
Chambersburg PA
CBRC102059150426
43195CB00007B/120